W9-COJ-914

Apr.'22 10 / 7 / 0

Incredible *Explorers*

Christopher Columbus

Discovering the Americas

Jack Connelly

Cavendish
Square

New York

Published in 2015 by Cavendish Square Publishing, LLC
243 5th Avenue, Suite 136, New York, NY 10016

Copyright © 2015 by Cavendish Square Publishing, LLC

First Edition

Website: cavendishsq.com

This publication represents the opinions and views of the author based on his or her personal experience, knowledge, and research. The information in this book serves as a general guide only. The author and publisher have used their best efforts in preparing this book and disclaim liability rising directly or indirectly from the use and application of this book.

CPSIA Compliance Information: Batch #WW15CSQ

All websites were available and accurate when this book was sent to press.

Library of Congress Cataloging-in-Publication Data

Connelly, Jack.
Christopher Columbus : discovering the Americas / Jack Connelly.
pages cm. — (Incredible explorers)
Includes index.
ISBN 978-1-50260-171-1 (hardcover) ISBN 978-1-50260-170-4 (ebook)
1. Columbus, Christopher—Juvenile literature. 2. Explorers—America—Biography—Juvenile literature. 3. Explorers—Spain—Biography—Juvenile literature. 4. America—Discovery and exploration—Spanish—Juvenile literature.
I. Title.

E111.C7785 2015
970.01'5092—dc23
[B]

2014029740

Editor: Andrew Coddington
Copy Editor: Cynthia Roby
Art Director: Jeffrey Talbot
Designer: Douglas Brooks
Photo Researcher: J8 Media
Senior Production Manager: Jennifer Ryder-Talbot
Production Editor: David McNamara

Contents

A Complicated Legacy

While history records his name as Christopher Columbus, he was probably known by different names during his time, depending on what country he was visiting. In his

Christopher Columbus has been both celebrated and reviled for generations.

homeland of Italy, he would have gone by his birth name, Christoforo Colombo. When he lived among the Portuguese, trying to learn all he could about sailing and the surrounding bodies of water, he was known as Christovao Colom. In Spain, it was Cristóbal Colón who tried to secure the patronage of the crown. Whatever name he was called, Columbus was constantly looking to use his sailing expertise in order to gain riches and status, as well as convert Native people to Christianity.

In fact, by 1492, after years of seeking support for his voyage from Spain's King Ferdinand and Queen Isabella, his terms, if his voyage succeeded, were high indeed. He clearly asked to be made governor of any land he "discovered" and to be given 10 percent of any gold or valuables found there. This would also include any earning from trade routes that might result from his efforts. His demands were high, but then so were his estimated risks.

Contrary to the modern myth that people living in **Renaissance** Italy believed that the world was flat, many people living in the fifteenth century understood that Earth was a sphere. They feared only what they did not understand, such as the conditions of the vast ocean near the equator, seas they believed "boiled" closest to the Tropics.

Columbus believed that the land his crew sighted on a turbulent day in 1492 was Asia, an area he called the **Indies**, which included Japan, China, Southeast Asia, and Indonesia, and that the Native people there were actually of Eastern descent. He was wrong. Columbus miscalculated because he misjudged Earth's circumference. He had no idea that a continent and another ocean, the Pacific, lay between him and his goal.

Columbus was naturally arrogant, and firmly entrenched in his belief that he and his crew had reached Asia. The region's people, whom he called "Indians" and described in his reports to the king and queen of Spain as "free with all they possess," were eager for the small trinkets he handed them. He hoped that they, in return, would fill his hands with gold.

If nothing else, his determination served him as well as his headstrong beliefs. Although he proved himself a master navigator at sea, Columbus was not as strong a leader on land. The settlements he began on the island of Hispaniola, now called Haiti, proved disastrous. His last voyages were marked with disgrace when he was barred from returning to the very settlements he had begun. As a result of ignoring the request of the Spanish monarchy to keep off the island of Hispaniola, his third return to Spain ended with the famous explorer bound in chains. Upon arriving in Spain after his last voyage, a now bitter Columbus found that his loyal supporter, Queen Isabella, was dying. Although Columbus had fallen from grace and lost his titles, he remained wealthy. Still, according to some historians, the respect that the Spanish monarchy had once had for his accomplishments was gone.

Columbus remains a controversial figure in the United States to this day. The nickname for the country, Columbia, is taken from the famous explorer, as is the name of the nation's capital: Washington, D.C., in which the D.C. stands for the District of Columbia. There is a national holiday in his honor every October, and many take great pride in celebrating his accomplishments. Others, however, feel that the enslavement, diseases, and **genocide** that his arrival brought to the Native peoples of North and South America are no reason to celebrate. However, the enormity of his accomplishments cannot be underestimated, as his explorations led to far-reaching changes for the history of multiple continents.

Chapter 1

The Early Life of Columbus

Genoa, located among the Ligurian Alps, Apennine Mountains, and Ligurian Sea, was a key port in Renaissance-era Italy. While the city was small during Columbus's time, it was a bustling seaport, second only

Although Columbus's hometown of Genoa was only a small city, it had a busy seaport. It hosted merchants and soldiers from around the known world.

to Venice in importance. The city served as a stopping point for merchants looking to do business and soldiers on their way to other countries.

Genoa was gloomy. Its streets were so narrow that riders on horseback rubbed their toes on the buildings' walls as they passed. Few grand structures had been built. Most of the city consisted of tiny homes that were dark and dank. Genoa's churches, built with arches in the Romanesque style, were short buildings with few windows. Even though it lacked elaborate architecture, the city had a reputation as one of the busiest markets on the western Mediterranean Sea. It was so famous for its trading, in fact, that the phrase *Genuensis ergo mercator*, which means "a Genoese, therefore a merchant," was common. The clash of weapons and screams of men were as much a part of the city as the shouts of sailors loading and unloading cargo. This was because Genoa, known for its seafaring and shipbuilding enterprises, was also envied for its prosperity, and many powers sought for control of it.

Despite its financial self-sufficiency, Genoa was often not strong enough to defend itself. The city and seaport was usually allied with another power, such as France or the Duchy of Milan. When these powers went to war, cannons fired at Genoa's walls and soldiers divided the city. When the outcome of the war was decided, Genoa might find itself under the protection of a different power. The constant shifting of political alliances and perils from raiders at sea could make Genoa a dangerous place to live.

Political factions constantly vied for power. These groups often made separate alliances with Aragon, a powerful kingdom that ruled much of the Mediterranean, and often brought outside conflicts into the lives of every person. Violence in Genoa's streets was common.

The House of Christopher Columbus

The home where Christopher grew up still exists in Genoa, just 50 yards (45.7 meters) from St. Andrew's city gate. Repaired and reconstructed many times over the centuries, it is now open to tourists and displays a small collection of items related to Christopher Columbus's life. Visitors who manage to find the out-of-the-way building see that the house would have been very dark inside due to its surroundings. The first floor was occupied by his

Christopher Columbus grew up in the second-story apartment of this small building in Genoa, Italy.

father's wool shop, and the family would have lived on the cramped second floor. A small plot out back had just enough space for a modest garden.

Columbus probably spent very little time in the small house when he was a boy, staying inside only when he helped his parents or when the city was under siege by rival city-states, which was a common occurrence in fifteenth-century Italy.

Christopher Columbus was born in 1451 into this hustling, thriving, and sometimes violent city. He learned to be observant at a very young age, and he tried to avoid trouble with other boys whose fathers had different political beliefs than his own father. Political violence was so common that Columbus's father's patron (financial supporter) was even stoned to death!

Looking to See the World

Like most other children in the city, Columbus was born into a family of merchants. His father and grandfather worked in the wool trade. They lived in the Portoria District's village of Mocónesi before Columbus was born, but later moved to Quinto, and then, finally, to Genoa. In the charged atmosphere of the densely populated city, Columbus's father, Domenico, settled down and established his business. It was there that he met and married Susanna Fontanarossa. Christopher was their first child. Other children came later: Giovanni, Bartolomeo, Giacomo, and Binachinetta. Although historians know that Giovanni died young, the others lived to adulthood. The two remaining brothers would accompany Columbus to the West Indies on his second voyage. He and Bartolomeo would later venture into a lucrative mapmaking business in Portugal, known for its small, compact maps called *portolanos*.

There were many things for young Christopher Columbus to see and do in Genoa. Behind the city stood the Alps, which, when climbed, offered solitude and a stunning view of the sea. Columbus thrived in the bustling activity rather than on the lonely mountain slopes, though. The port summoned Columbus, an inspired boy with an interest in learning.

The aromatic scent of exotic spices newly arrived in port must have excited him, too, along with the scent of fresh fish.

Several different Italian dialects were spoken by the sailors, as well as Spanish, English, and Portuguese. Columbus often sat for hours on the piers, watching the ships and the sailors who docked them. The merriment of the port made him dream of traveling. He wanted to see lands like Spain and England, and travel farther, possibly to Cathay (China).

Early Education

Columbus was educated in a primary school associated with the Wool Merchants Guild. He was instructed in **Catholicism**, arithmetic, and geography. As soon as he could, he learned to sail small fishing boats with other boys. He and his friends would fish all night long and then race home at dawn to be the first to bring their catch to market.

When Columbus was a boy, during the summers he stayed with his grandfather in Quinto to help with the grape harvest. Most people of medieval Italy never left their home city, but Columbus, like his parents, was not afraid of traveling. Most people believed that traveling was too dangerous.

Columbus was exceptional and independent in another way, too. In Quinto, a town with a beach rather than a port, he frequently went swimming in the ocean. This was an activity that was extremely unusual for his contemporaries, even other sailors. Columbus loved all aspects of the sea, though. He wanted to stare at it for days as it stretched to the horizon. He wanted to know every color, smell, and secret of the ocean. Swimming was just another way for him to be closer to his passion. The crashing of the waves, the changing play of colors there, and the cool salt spray on the rocks inspired his senses like nothing else.

When Columbus was eight years of age, his father Domenico decided to move the family to Savona, a city just west of Genoa.

The political faction that Domenico supported had lost power, and, as a result, his political appointment ended and his wool business was ruined. He felt he had to leave Genoa. In Savona, Domenico hoped to rebuild his business.

By the time Columbus was fifteen years of age, he was an accomplished sailor, experienced enough for his father to send him to nearby ports to gather wool and wine and to deliver finished cloth to buyers.

Columbus probably spent at least part of his teenage years sailing between Savona, Corsica, Provence, and other ports in northern Italy. He also worked in his father's shop and dreamt of the day he would see the world. He had finally achieved his goal of surrounding himself with the sea, but his voyages had always been short. Columbus wanted much more.

His first opportunity came in 1474. Genoese merchants on the island of Chios wanted weapons and supplies to protect them from the ships and soldiers of the Ottoman Empire, whose ships had already chased Genoese merchants from many of their ports. A fleet of five ships was sent to assist the Genoese on the island of Chios, and Columbus managed to secure himself a position on one of them, the *Roxanna*, a three-masted vessel.

Amazing Goods from the East

Columbus remained on Chios for one year, living independently for the first time. Chios had a port much like that of his native city, but unlike Genoa, the ships that came there brought more exotic goods than wine and wool. Strange spices such as nutmeg, mace, and cinnamon, marvelous perfumes, exotic silks, and pearls were all traded on a daily basis. The fantastic colors and unusual clothing of the people fired his imagination. Columbus could feel the call of the East from the near magical lands called

Cathay (China) and Cipango (Japan).

One scent dominated over all the others on Chios, the aroma of **mastic** trees. The trees' resin was used for drinks, for perfume, as a dessert, and even as medicine for upset stomachs. Exporting mastic brought great wealth to the people of Chios. Most of the exported mastic, though, went to the Turks of the Ottoman Empire, not to the Christians in Europe.

His time in Chios further inspired a young Christopher Columbus. He wanted to travel over the sea in order to obtain luxurious goods, including spices, mastic trees, and silks. He thought those products could be brought directly to Europe without having to go through the Turks. Columbus also knew that sailing the world and making this type of trade possible could bring him the fame and wealth he desired, a fame and wealth Columbus believed that God had ordained him to have.

Columbus was exposed to a wider world of trade during his time in the port city of Chios, Greece. Valuable trade goods were brought into Chios from Asia and the Middle East.

Chapter 2

Visions of Discovery

C olumbus was a devout Catholic. His son Ferdinand described him in *The History of the Life and Deeds of Christopher Columbus* as "so great an enemy of swearing and blasphemy that I never heard him utter any other oath than by

As he grew older, Columbus developed a singular goal: to explore the world.

St. Ferdinand." If he had to write anything, he always began by writing the words *Jesus cum Maria sit nobis in via*, a Latin phrase that means "May Jesus and Mary be with us on our way." Not surprisingly, Columbus, like most fifteenth-century sailors, never missed a chance to attend mass when he was in port and prayed often while aboard any ship. His son wrote in *Life and Deeds*, "He was so strict in matters of religion that for fasting and saying prayers he might have been taken for a member of a religious order."

Just as his first name carried special meaning for him because of its legend, so did his last. Although today we know him as Columbus, the Italian version of his name is Colombo, meaning "dove." Columbus was pleased at the thought that he, like the dove released by Noah on the ark, might go forth to find new land in the name of God.

Like his desire and religious motivations, Columbus was extraordinary in appearance, too. He was taller than most men, with a long nose and blue eyes. His hair, unlike most Italians, was strawberry blond, but it had turned white by the time he was thirty. His skin was pale and dotted with freckles. His appearance points to the probability that many of his ancestors came from northern Europe and had moved south into Italy over time.

Columbus was courageous, too, a characteristic, like discipline, that was necessary to pursue a lifetime of exploration. Part of his courage came from the belief he felt that God had chosen him to contribute something special from his life. By the time Columbus had traveled to the island of Chios, he was willing to work diligently toward his goals. He could be tactful and charming when he had to be, and incredibly patient.

Yet Columbus, despite his deep religious convictions and taste for simple living, sometimes ignored all tact and sensitivity. He had great confidence in himself and in God's trust in him, and these convictions could sometimes make him boastful and rude. While his youthful egoism was not considered a fault, later Columbus could not defend his pride with great leadership ability.

Getting to the East by Sailing... West?

Columbus was a dreamer, but he had the strength of will to achieve his dreams. Despite his son's exaggerations about Columbus's schooling in *Life and Deeds*, historians have reported that the expert navigator had little formal education. According to Daniel J. Boorstin's book, *The Discoverers*: "[Columbus] had no formal schooling where he might have learned Italian, and when by his own efforts he became literate, he wrote Castilian, which was the favorite language of the educated classes on the Iberian Peninsula, including Portugal." Columbus also needed to learn specialized skills such as cartography (mapmaking) and geography, unlike most educated men his age.

Fortunately, Columbus was never too proud to ask questions and display his ignorance before more learned men. He had a copy of a letter from a famous Florentine cartographer and astronomer of the day, Paolo dal Pozzo Toscanelli, in which the mapmaker proposed sailing to Asia across the **Ocean Sea**. At the time of Columbus, the Atlantic Ocean was known as the Ocean Sea, since no other ocean had been identified. Toscanelli wrote in the letter, "Directly opposite them [Africa and Europe] to the west is shown the beginning of the Indies with the islands and places you may reach." Toscanelli's map incorrectly showed Japan only 4,000 miles (6,437 kilometers) west of the Canary Islands, when the actual distance was more than three times greater than he believed—some 12,000 miles (19,312 km).

Inspired by Explorers Past

Among the many accounts of explorations Columbus read, those of Marco Polo proved particularly exciting to him. An Italian like Columbus, Polo had gone to China using a land route from 1271 to 1295. Polo traveled through Asia Minor, Persia, Central Asia, and Mongolia.

After spending more than twenty years in Asia, Marco Polo had returned to Italy with tales of its splendid gold cities and the lavish court of the Mongol emperor Kublai Khan. Polo's accounts of Asia's wealth were so fantastic that many of his contemporaries accused him of fabricating much, if not all, of it. Polo's journal was published in 1298 in a book titled The Travels of Marco Polo. Columbus, it is said, carried a copy of Polo's book with him on his journey across the Atlantic.

Columbus's predecessor, Marco Polo, spent decades living in Asia. When he returned to Europe, he brought with him stories of incredible wealth and exotic cultures.

Inspired by Polo, Columbus was determined to reach this spectacular land by sea. The land route to Cathay was limited because of the Turks. If any European wanted to go there, he would have to travel around the coast of Africa or across the Ocean Sea.

The Portuguese had made many attempts to reach Asia by going around Africa but had not thought about sailing west. Diego Cão made two voyages along the west coast of Africa in the 1480s, years before both Bartolomeu Dias and Vasco da Gama. Dias returned to Lisbon in 1488, around the same time that Columbus arrived there, too, again seeking sponsorship from the king to sail to the Indies. When Dias returned, triumphantly reporting having finally successfully rounded the coast of Africa, Columbus knew that his chances of gaining sponsorship were again slim. With this, he became obsessed with the idea that going west was the best way—if not the only way—that traveling to Asia could be accomplished.

Sailing to England

Though he became obsessed with traveling west in order to go east, Columbus was careful to gather evidence of a navigable route. He often questioned sailors and merchants about what they had seen. While his heart burned to sail west, he knew he had to bide his time. To begin his voyage, he first needed financial support and other assistance. To get that support, he needed solid evidence that his plan was possible. Biding his time also meant gaining more experience at sea for the long journey. In the summer of 1476, Columbus sailed out of the Mediterranean Sea bound for England with a convoy of five Genoese ships laden with goods.

Once the convoy Columbus was part of made it past the Strait of Gibraltar, Columbus saw the ocean for the first time in his life. He believed it was the only ocean, and that he would be able to reach Asia by sailing on it. Before heading west, he planned on gaining the sailing experience by heading north to England. He did not know that his journey would not lead him to his planned destination.

Chapter 3

Exploring
His Horizons

Columbus was part of the crew of a convoy of five ships looking to deliver cargo to England. The voyage represented Columbus's first experience sailing the open ocean, but it did not last long. As they headed toward

The caravel was a popular form of ship used by explorers during Columbus's time. It was sturdy and designed to withstand the rough waters of the open ocean.

Cape St. Vincent, located on the southwest corner of Portugal, enemy ships quickly surrounded them. Thirteen Franco-Portuguese ships under the command of the naval leader Guillaume de Casenove attacked Columbus's convoy. Two of the five ships managed to escape, and Columbus's ships sank four of the Franco-Portuguese fleet. The other three ships of the convoy were sunk, including the one Columbus was on, the *Bechalla*.

Many of the shipwrecked men from the Franco-Portuguese and Genoese ships drowned, short of a few who were only injured, including Columbus. Thanks to the time spent swimming as a youth, he was an athletic swimmer. He spent the entire night clutching an oar and paddling to shore until he reached the Portuguese town of Lagos, where local fishermen met him. Columbus viewed the shipwreck as an act of God and later wrote in a letter to Spain's King Ferdinand, "God miraculously sent me here."

From Lagos, Columbus traveled to Lisbon, the capital of Portugal, where he briefly joined his brother, Bartolomeo, a cartographer, before returning to Genoa. When he next left for England, he traveled without mishap, but his brief stay in Lagos, the Portuguese center of sea navigation, was important for the development of his quest. It was in Lagos that Columbus learned some Portuguese, Castilian, and Latin, as well as the mathematics and astronomy needed for successful sea navigation.

Exploring Farther North

Now in England, Columbus's keen eye discovered clues that the world was larger than he had ever supposed. In English ports, he saw an abundance of cod and salmon, seen occasionally in Genoa, but then only salted and dried. Yet in England, there were markets with vast amounts of both kinds. Columbus was told that the fish were found in the cold waters of the North Sea and from the distant land they called Ultima Thule, a place now known as Iceland. To a fifteenth-century explorer, Ultima Thule was the closest to the northernmost territory of the known world. Columbus was intrigued. He wanted to learn more about this mysterious land in the north. He left England for Ireland and then joined a crew on a fleet bound for Iceland.

Portugal's History of Exploration

Lagos's fine harbor had seen many expeditions leave to explore the far reaches of the known world, such as those sent forth by Portugal's Prince Henry the Navigator. Like Columbus, Prince Henry was obsessed with the exploration of the Far East and by his desire to gain its exotic treasures. If Columbus had not heard of Prince Henry before, he certainly heard about him from the Lagos fishermen, who loved to tell stories about this pioneer who, according to some historians, started a school of navigation in Portugal, earning him the nickname "the Navigator."

Prince Henry the Navigator was a hero to Portuguese sailors. He is reported to have started a school of navigation.

Through his travels, Prince Henry popularized a new type of ship. The **caravel**, a lighter and faster vessel than any other contemporary ship, and the same type that would later be used by Columbus on his own voyages, was a sturdy, small vessel well suited to handle the rough Ocean Sea.

Iceland proved to be unlike any place Columbus had ever seen. Huge white glaciers glinted blue in the sun, while smoking mountains poured lava into the turbulent sea. Columbus was fascinated with the bleak, treeless landscape filled with bogs, grasses, and geysers that spat boiling water into the air.

The Norse settlers who had **colonized** Iceland had, hundreds of years earlier, also found a land to the west they called Vinland. (Today, Vinland is believed to have been either Labrador or Newfoundland.) Columbus never mentioned Vinland in his carefully collected list of evidence to prove that land existed west of Europe, so he probably never heard of Vinland. Still, Vinland would not have interested Columbus because he was seeking only Asian lands.

Even though Columbus did not hear about Vinland in his travels to Iceland, he did gain one important fact: The ancient Greeks had been wrong in their belief that no one could live in extreme northern regions. Columbus now knew this was false having visited Iceland. If the Greeks had been wrong about the extremity of northern living conditions, what other facts had they reported inaccurately? After his visit to Iceland, Columbus returned to Lisbon and settled there. He knew that he could never attain his dream of sailing across the Atlantic Ocean by remaining in Italy. If he really wanted to sail west over the Ocean Sea, he would have to remain in Spain or Portugal where monarchs were interested in exploration and could supply the money needed to fund any voyages there.

Marrying into Nobility

While in Lisbon, Columbus met a young woman named Felipa Perestrello Moniz. His interest in Felipa went beyond mere attraction, however. She was of noble blood, though her

Christopher Columbus married a noblewoman named Felipa Perestrello Moniz. He hoped marrying into one of Portugal's oldest noble families would help him secure support for his voyage.

family had become impoverished. Her mother's family was one of the oldest noble families in all of Portugal. Marrying a noblewoman, even a poor one, would increase Columbus's chances of acquiring wealth and his own royal title.

There was another reason that his marriage to Felipa was noteworthy. This was because her late father had been the governor of Porto Santo, a tiny island in the Ocean Sea, she had access to important documents, including maps. Columbus's son wrote in *Life and Deeds*, "His mother-in-law gave him the writings and maps which her husband had left her. They excited [him] all the more, informing him of other voyages that the Portuguese were making."

After marrying Felipa, Columbus moved to Porto Santo, where his son Diego was born. While on the island, he spent his time studying the extensive library left by Felipa's father and walking the beaches of the nearby island of Madeira. Columbus often wandered the western beaches, hoping to find some trace of lands far to the west washed up in the debris. He would sometimes find evidence such as strange seeds then unknown in Europe.

Columbus did more than just wander the shoreline. He took ships to many ports, including Elmira, which is in present-day Ghana, Africa. Columbus later wrote to Spain's King Ferdinand that the climate near the equator was mild, much different from the Torrid Zone described by the ancient Greeks. He had first-hand experience that some equatorial regions were not too hot for people to live in after all.

The Europeans were more concerned with African gold, a dream Columbus had as well. He spent much energy asking questions about the areas plentiful with precious elements. Could gold be found near mountains or in streams? By learning these clues, he expected to find gold in the Indies when he finally sailed there. With his newfound knowledge, he often sailed between Santo Porto, Elmira, the Canary Islands, and Portugal, learning everything he could about the prevailing wind patterns, the current, and the tides.

Columbus is noteworthy for several reasons: He discovered the original westward sea passage from Europe to North America, a passage that sailors still use today because of its efficiency, and he did it without the aid of the traditional navigational equipment that was developed years later. His instinct was his only safe-guard, other than the quadrant, a simple instrument that determines altitude, and a basic magnetic compass. Still more remarkable was that Columbus was able to return to his original destinations in future voyages.

While Columbus continued to dream of reaching land by sailing west from Europe, he also continued to sail around Europe and Africa, building his experience as a sailor in preparation for the greatest voyage of his life. He also read as much as he could about the possibility of distant lands, lands he wanted to reach and claim for one of the European nations.

Chapter 4

Ferdinand and Isabella

I n 1485, Columbus's wife died of unknown causes. It was in the wake of this family tragedy that Columbus decided to travel to Portugal with his five-year-old son, Diego. Having built up an incredible amount of sailing experience, he believed he was ready to cross the

Columbus petitioned King Ferdinand and Queen Isabella of Spain for funding to explore the west. His requests were unsuccessful for years until they finally agreed to fund three ships and their crews.

Ocean Sea and look for his oft-dreamed-of distant lands. To do that however, he needed the backing of a monarch with the financial and political power to make the journey happen.

Still, King João II of Portugal was convinced that the only way to reach Asia was by traveling around the coast of Africa. Although not one of the Portuguese fleets had made the journey successfully, every expedition extended farther than those before. The king was certain that Portugal would soon have a trade route to Asia, and it would most certainly not involve sailing west across a vast stretch of ocean! To King João II, traveling around the coast of Africa was much safer than heading across unknown seas, especially after Bartolomeu Dias rounded the continent in 1488.

Columbus was sorely disappointed when the king disagreed with his proposition. After all, he had spent years documenting his evidence, including Toscanelli's map, which clearly showed Japan just a few thousand miles west of Portugal.

Knowing the king would not change his mind, Columbus decided to visit the Spanish monarchs instead. He and Diego stepped ashore at the Spanish city of Palos and visited La Rabida, a church near the port. Columbus, who always went to mass at the end of a voyage, was also searching for lodging. He knew that a room at a church would be safer for a young boy like Diego than staying at one of the town's inns.

Support from the Church

At La Rabida, Columbus met Father Antonio de Marchena, a man who watched the stars. When Columbus learned that one of the friars at the church studied astronomy, too, he was very excited. Together they talked late into the night. Columbus explained everything he had learned about Iceland, Africa, and Porto Santo, and detailed his evidence. Father Marchena was so enthusiastic about Columbus's efforts that he decided to support his ambitions.

Diego was sent to live with the local group of Spanish monks. After the boy was seen safely away, and with Marchena as his guide, Columbus traveled to the city of Alcala de Henares near Madrid. Here, Marchena managed to get him invited to the royal court. On January 20, 1486, Columbus was ushered for the first time into the presence of the monarchs of Spain, King Ferdinand and Queen Isabella.

ROUND EARTH

It is a common story that Christopher Columbus's crew was worried that they would sail so far west that they would eventually fall off the side of a flat Earth, and that Columbus was the first person to believe that Earth was round and not flat. While it's a fun story to tell, Christopher Columbus was not the first person to hypothesize that Earth was round. In fact, the idea that Earth is actually round dates back as far as the sixth century BCE, when early Greek travelers noted that the position of stars changed based on one's location, and that the height of objects changed based on distance. By the fifteeth century CE, most people understood that the world was a sphere and that sailing west should, ultimately, get one to Asia.

Although most people agreed that Earth was round, what could not be agreed on was its actual size. No one was certain, even though it was frequently debated among learned men. Although Columbus and his crew were confident that their westerly route would eventually lead to the East, what was unknown was how long it would take to get there, if they even got there. Ships travelling along Africa's coast could remain close to the shore for the entire length of the trip, whereas traveling west would ultimately mean leaving the shore for an unknown length of time. In a small wooden ship, leaving the sight of land was a very risky undertaking.

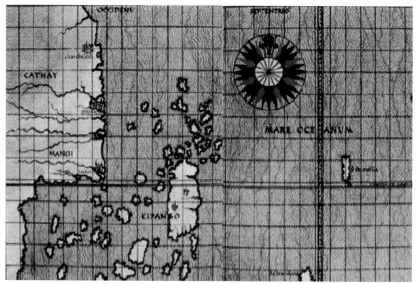

One of the pieces of evidence Columbus used to persuade the king and queen was Toscanelli's map, which positioned Cathay (China) and Cipango (Japan) just a few thousand miles west of Europe.

Although the king and queen were curious and listened intently while Columbus spoke of what he called his Enterprise of the Indies, their advisers told them that what he proposed was impossible.

Yet the fact that the king and queen had been curious gave Columbus hope that they could later be persuaded. With this in mind he remained in Spain, following the court from city to city. He fell in love with a peasant woman named Beatriz who became the mother of his second son, Ferdinand. He refined his proposal and studied further to gather the additional evidence that he needed for his success.

Finally, in 1489, Queen Isabella sent for Columbus. Although not prepared to finance an expedition, she wanted to learn more about his "Enterprise of the Indies." Moreover, she wanted Columbus to live at court so he could remain nearby. The queen could do nothing while her husband, King Ferdinand, was away fighting the **Moors** (Spanish **Muslims**), but she promised to address it with him after he returned. Columbus was thrilled to have gained her interest. He lived with the Spanish court while he awaited the king's consent. The queen also helped financially, too, with a small monthly allowance.

The fighting that the queen had thought would end shortly lasted more than two years. By January 1492, a special council was called in the hopes that Columbus's plan would be taken more seriously. However, the council still claimed that it would be impossible to sail to Asia by crossing the Western Ocean. Columbus was sent away from the court. His years in Spain had seemingly been for nothing.

Now completely dejected, Columbus thought of sailing to France to visit the French monarch, King Charles VIII, where he thought his chances of gaining sponsorship would be greater. However, Columbus had noble friends in Spain who did not waver in their support. They continued to pressure the Spanish monarchs and even presented a plan by which the city of Palos would be largely responsible for the finances of the voyage. Palos was already subject to a fine due to smuggling; now the fine would be applied to Columbus's venture.

Approval for His Plan

King Ferdinand, eager for whatever territory could be gained from the voyage, was convinced of Columbus's ability to sail west over the vast stretch of turbulent and uncharted ocean. Queen Isabella didn't hesitate. She sent out a messenger to locate the headstrong explorer. At last he had permission to sail, and the paperwork required to gain ships, supplies, and sailors was under way. Columbus, now forty-one, left Palos bound for the Indies across the Atlantic Ocean on August 3, 1492.

Two of his three ships, the *Niña* and the *Pinta*, were the small, sturdy caravels popularized by Prince Henry. A third ship, the *Santa Maria*, was the flagship of the fleet. It was a **nao**, a merchant ship, and larger than the caravels. Compared to the caravels, the *Santa Maria* was slow and clumsy.

Before Columbus could sail into unknown waters, he needed to stop his fleet in Gomera, near the Canary Islands. It was the westernmost known harbor and the last place to gather supplies before facing the breadth of the rough, gray seas. While at Gomera, the ships took on firewood, salted, or preserved, meat, and fresh water. The sailors, who had just witnessed a volcanic eruption on the island, were very frightened, but Columbus calmed their spirits.

The ships left Gomera's port on September 6 with approximately ninety men, most of whom were Spanish. Some were criminals who had agreed to sail in return for freedom, since most sailors refused to make a journey they considered perilous and deadly. No one knew that Columbus was an experienced navigator, and few wanted to sail at all. Even those who did were skeptical. Sailing was a risky undertaking, and the captain of any ship had to be courageous, talented, and able to lead his crew and navigate his vessel through treacherous waters, rocks, and storms. The Spanish sailors did not trust Columbus with such an important task.

Columbus's first had to pass through an area known as the Sargasso Sea. This is an area of the Atlantic Ocean where seaweed accumulates and sea life such as worms, crabs, fish, and insects gather in abundance. Columbus may have heard about it from other sailors. The Sargasso Sea changes in shape and location each year and is often difficult to navigate.

By September 16, Columbus's ships first encountered what he called "weeds." The following day, the seaweed was thicker, and by September 21, it was so thick that "the sea seemed completely curdled with it," as Columbus wrote in his ship log. Their slow progress through the Sargasso Sea continued until the second week in October, each day marked by increasing and decreasing amounts of debris.

Dead Reckoning

Columbus's sailors were becoming nervous. Not only were they the first Europeans to cross this section of sea, they felt unusually uneasy about sailing so far from port. It was now more than a month since they had touched land, and the behavior of the winds and the tides were unlike anything they had experienced. Most of the crewmen were eager to return home.

During his years of documenting prevailing wind patterns, Columbus discovered they blow east to west in certain **latitudes**. Consequently, when he wanted to go west, he chose the latitude of the winds that consistently blew in that direction, known to modern sailors as the **trade winds**. His crew, who did not know that he wanted to choose a different latitude on the way home, were worried about trying to return across the ocean with the winds against them. There were disagreements among the crew, frequently breaking into physical fights.

Columbus, however, was quite sure of where he was and of how to return home. In fact, he was a master **dead reckoner**. This means that he could estimate where his ship was located by calculating its speed and the length of time since its last known position. During the time of Columbus, sailors could determine latitude—that is, how far north of the equator they were—but they could not determine **longitude**, which was their exact point east or west. By utilizing dead-reckoning skills, ship captains could estimate, sometimes quite accurately, where they were positioned.

Unfortunately, dead reckoning was still only guessing. The longer one had been on a journey, the tougher it was to pinpoint an accurate position. The speed of the ship may have changed too many times, and the sailors responsible for turning the hourglass may have forgotten once or twice. Columbus somehow could compensate for many of these slight and unpredictable changes. He was one of the most able navigators ever known when it came to dead-reckoning skills.

Finally, intent on gaining a reward set aside by the king and queen for the first sailor who spotted land, a lookout on the *Pinta* sighted sand dunes on October 12 and cried out, "*Tierra! Tierra!*" (Land! Land!) At long last, Columbus had completed the first part of his quest. He had crossed the Atlantic Ocean and landed near what he believed was Asia. (Later, Columbus took the reward money for himself, and the sailor got nothing.)

Since Columbus firmly believed he was near Asia, he had no reason to make any particular note of his first landfall, a place historians now believe was either Watling Island (San Salvador Island) or another in the Bahamas. Lately, however, many scholars have disputed this assumption.

The theory is that those who assume Watling Island is correct do not account for ocean current. If one combines Columbus's data with the trade winds and the ocean currents, then Columbus's landfall was most likely at a small island called Samana Cay. Still, other scholars commonly dispute this theory, too.

Ultimately the exact point of Columbus's first landfall is a smaller issue. Columbus and his crew had made it to a New World. Columbus's years of preparation, study, sailing, and searching for financing had finally paid off. He could silence the doubters who thought it was impossible to cross the Ocean Sea, now known as the Atlantic Ocean.

Chapter 5

Reaching New Lands

Before disembarking the ship, Columbus and his crew first sailed around the island in order to discover the safest landing spot. Shortly after dawn, they set foot on the island. Columbus and several of his crewmembers kneeled down and kissed the

Columbus and his crew made landfall on October 12, 1492. They had discovered the New World.

ground in joy. Most thanked God for the successful journey.

The royal standard, or flag, of Spain was unfurled on the beach. Two other flags, one marked with an 'F' for King Ferdinand, the other marked with a 'Y' for Queen Isabella, whose name was often spelled Ysabel, were also planted in the sand. Columbus asked the others to officially witness that he took possession of the island for Spain.

The people native to the area, who did not know their island had just been claimed in the name of Spanish monarchs thousands of miles away, watched the Europeans with curious eyes. Columbus, having noticed the islanders, too, was just as curious. They wore no clothes and had no metal tools or weapons except sticks with sharp fish teeth on the ends. Columbus, in his eagerness to convert these strange people to Christianity, decided to take six of the Native people with him so that he could teach them to speak Spanish and be good Catholics.

Looking for Riches

Though the people he encountered did not match the known descriptions of the people of Asia, Columbus called them "Indians" because he believed he had landed in India. The fabulous cities of gold, where spices and precious items could be bought in markets similar to ones on Chios, must be nearby, he thought.

Despite their cordial meeting, the Europeans and the indigenous people had misunderstandings. Columbus noticed one person wearing a small plug of gold jewelry and assumed there must be more of the precious metal. The Native people indicated that great quantities of gold could be found farther south, but they knew only about searching streams for gold nuggets, not nearly the amount of gold Columbus wanted. He was looking for mines that would yield tons of the precious metal.

Columbus also noted that the Native people would give anything they had for mere trinkets, but in a land where metal was an unknown substance, small tools or sharpened knives were anything but trinkets. A scrap of fabric or an old button might mean little to Columbus, but to the Native people these objects were new and unusual. In his 1493 letter to King Ferdinand and Queen Isabella, Columbus related his findings about the Native people: "They are artless and so free with all they possess. They are content with whatever little thing of whatever kind may be given to them."

Columbus began to understand that it would be easy to take advantage of the Native peoples' giving nature. He forbade his men to trade anything without his permission so he could be certain that the Native people would receive items of value in exchange for their cotton and gold.

Reaching Cuba

After deciding to head south, Columbus again boarded with his crew and a few Native people, and kept his fleet moving. At each island, they met more Native people who assured him that gold could be found farther south on a larger island named Cuba. Finally, on October 27, Columbus sighted Cuba. Believing it was Japan, he wrote in the ship's log, "I think it must be Cipango, judging from the information which the Indians I have with me provide."

Yet Columbus could find no fabulous cities of gold. Still, he would not admit that he had not found Asia. His stubborn attitude had served him well over the years, but now, his hard headedness kept him from seeing the truth. As far as Columbus was concerned, the only land west of Europe was Asia; therefore, he must have found a sea route to Asia. Marco Polo had written of the thousands of islands off the eastern coast of Cathay, so it was natural to first stumble upon them. Columbus felt certain that the wonderfully rich cities and exotic markets he had not found awaited him beyond his recent discoveries.

Thinking he was describing Japan, Columbus wrote of the wonders of Cuba, describing its high, beautiful mountains. The trees and spices of Cuba, and later, Hispaniola, enchanted Columbus. Since he had not yet found a source of gold, he needed other news to report to Spain. In doing so, he noted the thick forest, packed with straight hardwood trees useful for many things, from building houses to ships. He used his remarkable sense of smell to identify fine spices, including what he believed were mastic trees. Recalling how Chios had made itself rich with mastic resin, Columbus was excited to fantasize about the revenue Spain could acquire through this one item alone. Columbus's nose failed him in this regard, though. In reality, he had not found a new source of the valuable resin. Columbus was accurate, however, about the value of cotton. He noted that the Native people cultivated it, and rightly figured that it could be a great source of revenue for Spain.

Despite his inability to find a source of gold, Columbus continued sailing around the Caribbean searching for it. On every island, he found only a few small nuggets usually worn as jewelry, but nothing more. The golden lands of Cathay and Cipango still eluded him.

By Christmas Eve, Columbus's nao, the *Santa Maria*, ran aground on a section of underwater coral off the coast of Hispaniola. Before his crew realized their situation, their ship was bouncing up and down on the razor sharp coral with every wave.

Sailors on the *Niña* were unable to free the vessel from the reef. The sharp coral punctured the *Santa Maria's* bottom, and, as the tide lowered, more coral scraped its hull. Finally, the ship was destroyed.

The First Settlement

Many of the men of the *Santa Maria* could not fit onto both the *Niña* and the *Pinta*, so Columbus decided to found a settlement on the island of Hispaniola. Guacanagari, the chief of the

Taíno—an Arawak people who were one of the major indigenous peoples of the Caribbean—was friendly. With supplies collected from the ships, thirty-nine men stayed to build the settlement of La Navidad, Spanish for "Christmas."

Columbus sailed away from the first European settlement on January 4, 1493, having left them with enough goods, weapons, and food for one year. Surely, as he set out toward Europe in the east, he felt he had accomplished a great deal and deserved any reward he would be given. Not only had he found a sea route to the Indies for Spain but also Native people who were **pagans** and could be converted to Catholicism. Moreover, Columbus had established the first Spanish town in the West Indies.

Columbus faced continual challenges, though. The crossing back to Europe was much worse than anything the ships had faced before. Eventually, the *Niña* and the *Pinta* were separated by a terrible storm. At several points, both the crew and Columbus were certain the ships would not survive. As a safeguard, Columbus went so far as to take a copy of his ship's log, place it in a barrel, and throw it overboard. He hoped that if his ship were to sink, the document that detailed his journey might wash up on a Portuguese or Spanish beach. Then his discoveries and the existence of La Navidad would be known, even if he were dead.

Although the two ships were separated, each managed to reach Palos, Spain, on the same day, March 15, 1493. Columbus was onboard the *Niña*, which reached the city first, but the *Pinta* followed that afternoon. It was a stunning return, as most residents of the city never expected the ships to make it back from their journey. Columbus and his crew were celebrated as heroes, and many residents joined Columbus and his fellow sailors when they went immediately to mass to give thanks for a successful voyage home.

Chapter 6

The Spanish in the New World

erdinand and Isabella were ecstatic about Columbus's return. Even before they received the hero, they sent a letter to him that granted Columbus his official titles. When he appeared before the king and queen, Columbus would be

Columbus returned to Spain and presented King Ferdinand and Queen Isabella with proof of his journey, including plants, animals, spices, gold, and Native people.

the Admiral of the Ocean Sea and the viceroy and governor of the islands of the Indies.

The Spanish court was in Barcelona when Columbus arrived, so he traveled there with what he had brought back as proof of his discovery: parrots, spices, plants, gold trinkets, and several of the islands' Native people.

Returning to the New World

The king and queen listened as Columbus explained everything that had happened since he had departed the previous year. He told the monarchs that he knew he could find more gold and other treasures if he had additional supplies, ships, and time to search.

Ferdinand and Isabella were convinced. They treated Columbus almost as if he were a king himself. The grand cardinal of Spain even gave Columbus a food taster, which indicated how he was admired and respected. Only very important people who were in danger of being poisoned were granted food tasters. Columbus was now thought of as an aristocrat.

A mere six months later, the Admiral of the Ocean Sea set sail again, still anticipating wealth and further honors. This time he was in charge of seventeen ships—three naos and fourteen caravels, including the *Niña* from his first voyage. Besides sailors, Columbus embarked with craftsmen, priests, soldiers, and even horses, in anticipation of expanding the settlement at La Navidad.

After exploring the coastlines of several islands, including Puerto Rico, Columbus turned his fleet toward La Navidad, confident that he could expand the settlement for Spain and then continue his search for gold, spices, and other treasures.

The sight that greeted Columbus's crew when they returned to La Navidad was one they had never imagined. The settlement had been burned, and the thirty-nine men left behind after the

Santa Maria was destroyed were dead. The Taíno who lived in the area told Columbus of a raid on their village and on the Spanish by the Caribs. Caribs, a different group of indigenous people, were increasingly fierce. According to some Taíno, Caribs often cooked and ate their enemies. The Caribs were believed to be cannibals, but some historians dispute this belief.

THE DESTRUCTION OF LA NAVIDAD

Historians have consistently speculated on the events at La Navidad. The Spanish who had been left behind were sailors, not farmers or carpenters. They wanted to find gold, not establish a town, but the local Native people had little to offer them. The Spanish crewmen, who had been led by Columbus to believe the area was full of wealth, were unhappy to be stranded on a foreign coast with only a few strange, if friendly, Native people for company. Most likely, they argued among themselves and with the Native people, and generally behaved badly toward each other and their Taíno neighbors.

Word of the arrival of the Spanish had most likely reached the Caribs, who lived in the mountains rather than on the beach like the Taíno. Warlike and aggressive, the Caribs probably believed that raiding the settlement of foreigners who had metal tools was a good idea. The Spanish could not defend themselves against an organized raid. The Taíno, who had been friendly with the Spanish, suffered along with the Europeans before the Caribs returned to their mountain homes.

Columbus was shocked and saddened to hear that his crew was dead. However, instead of grieving, he quickly ordered the men in his fleet to look for another site for a settlement. He must have realized that the fate of La Navidad would keep his men from trusting him as they had before. He had told the king and queen that the men he had left behind were living with friendly Native people. This was not entirely true. Many Native people were friendly, but not all of them were eager to trust foreigners. Those who had come with Columbus had not counted on fighting. They only wanted to search for gold and trade goods with friendly Native people.

In order to maintain the spirit of his crew, Columbus had to found a new settlement. His men were afraid and growing doubtful. To calm them, Columbus tried to make for a harbor he remembered from his previous trip, but the trade winds prevented him from sailing there. Instead, he went ashore on January 2, 1494, at the first stretch of safe coastline he could find, where the Yaque del Norte River flowed into the sea. The new settlement would be called La Isabela.

Building La Isabela

The new colonists first erected a church, made of stone, which was finished in one month. They also built a sanctuary and a protective wall around it. Every public building in La Isabela would be made of stone. The Native people would not get a second chance to burn the Spanish out of the Indies.

The colonists, priests, and craftsmen who made the second journey were better at building and organizing a settlement than the first group had been. By April 24, they had already assembled public buildings and private homes, and they had an official mayor.

Meanwhile, Columbus continued searching for gold. He sent members of his crew to search the island's interior, and they returned with several gold nuggets. Columbus, now excited by their discovery, sent twelve of his seventeen ships back to Spain with the pieces and the promise that there would soon be more.

He went to see the area where the gold had been found. Columbus collected nearly fifty pounds of it from the Native people and then left his soldiers nearby to build a fort.

The Native people were frightened of the horses, so Columbus made sure the animals stayed at the fort to keep them afraid and under control. After the tragedy of La Navidad, Columbus wanted no more bloodshed.

Columbus returned to La Isabela and then departed to further explore the Caribbean. He sailed along the southern coast of Cuba and discovered an island he named Jamaica—after its native name, Xaymaca. All the while, he continued to search for the mainland that he strongly believed would bring him to Asia.

By now, he had seen so many islands he was certain he was somewhere near the Malay Peninsula, just east of Asia. Therefore, he believed that Cuba must be the Malay Peninsula and not Cipango after all. However he did not travel all the way around Cuba, merely an additional 50 miles (80.5 km), so he believed it was part of a mainland, not an island. Historians believe that Columbus did not want to accept the possibility that Cuba was, in fact, another island. Like his quest for gold, he continued to cherish his dream of reaching Asia. If Cuba were just another island, then Asia was farther away than he thought, a disappointment he could not bear.

Columbus sailed back to La Isabela, reaching the settlement by September 29. By this time, additional ships had arrived from Europe carrying women and children. The town was growing quickly. The gardens planted by the first colonists had produced amazing amounts of food. Columbus's son Ferdinand later wrote in *Life and Deeds*, "[Columbus] found some of the melons already ripe, although barely two months had passed since planting. Similarly, the watermelons were ready after twenty days . . ."

Unfortunately, the Spanish could not exist on fruit alone. Fish was abundant in the surrounding water, but most of the colonists did not know how to take advantage of such a bounty. In the hot climate, people did not want to exert much energy, and most were already malnourished. Those who were the weakest grew sick early, some from syphilis, others from swine fever or other diseases such as malaria. La Isabela quickly became a hospital for the Spanish colonists.

Columbus ordered everyone to work in the fields. He urged them to build waterwheels to harness the Rio Yaque's energy for a mill. The soldiers disliked being told to do the work of farmers and carpenters, especially when the farmers and carpenters were idle. No one had enough food to eat, and La Isabela was already in trouble.

Difficulties at the Colony

Columbus was truly lost. He had no gift for leadership, especially when it came to making decisions on land. His actions on board a ship, where his word was law, were accepted much differently. While sailing, his confidence and enthusiasm fueled the morale of the crew, and his strengths were unparalleled. Yet he had no idea how to save the endangered colony. People were dying, no one would work, and the soldiers were on the verge of rebellion.

Columbus reacted cruelly. He ordered some to be whipped, and others were hanged. When one of the Catholic priests protested, Columbus kept him from eating. Eventually, hunger forced the priest to agree to Columbus's tactics.

Understandably, the colonists were starting to hate their stubborn leader. He had promised wealth and spices, but all they had seen was endless labor, hunger, sickness, and death. To keep from working, some of the Spanish were kidnapping people native to the island as slaves. The once friendly Taíno were learning to distrust the settlers. Mutinous colonists even commandeered some of the remaining caravels and headed back to Spain. Everywhere Columbus turned, it seemed his dreams were ruined.

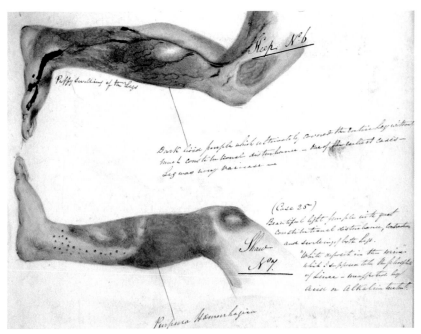

The colonists at La Isabella suffered from many diseases, including those resulting from malnutrition such as scurvy. Scurvy causes the gums to be soft, teeth to fall out, skin to be easily bruised, and soreness. It can be fatal.

Meanwhile, relations with the Native people became so hostile that the Spanish and the Caribs went to war in Hispaniola in 1495. The Carib leader, Caonabó, gathered many tribes to assist him, including some Taíno. Any Taíno man who refused to help Caonabó against the Spanish was murdered. Only their chief, Guacanagari, survived because he ran away.

On March 27, the first battle was fought. Caonabó and his men killed forty diseased Spanish soldiers and surrounded the fort that Columbus had started. The siege lasted a month before Caonabó decided he couldn't starve the soldiers into submission.

Caonabó surveyed the settlement and realized that all the soldiers were back at the fort. He thought he would be able to defeat the colonists easily, probably because most were already ill. However, Guacanagari remained loyal to Columbus. He reached the explorer while Columbus was in bed with severe arthritis

The capture of the Carib chief Caonabó marked the beginning of Spanish dominance over the Natives of the Caribbean.

and told him about the raid. Columbus was able to assemble enough men to rout Caonabó's forces.

Caonabó was tricked and captured by Columbus and members of his crew. He had never seen iron manacles before and was convinced that European kings wore these metal bracelets as a sign of nobility. Of course, once the manacles were on his wrists, Caonabó was taken prisoner, and his rebellion was over.

Now with little resistance, the Spanish were able to dominate the Native people and force them to pay **tribute** in the form of gold. Many of the Native people did not have any gold, so they left their homes in order to escape the Spanish soldiers, as well as their horses and dogs. Scores of Native people committed suicide, while others were captured and brought to Spain as slaves. While reaching the New World began an era of prosperity for the Spanish, it began an era of misery for the Native people.

Chapter 7

Troubles for Columbus

Columbus began his second voyage from the New World to Spain in March of 1496. When he arrived, he did not meet the same excitement and fanfare that had characterized his first return. Other settlers who had come from the

As time went on, it became more apparent that Columbus had not landed in Asia but on a whole new continent, forcing people to reevaluate how they imagined the world.

New World ahead of Columbus had shared grisly tales of slavery and torture of indigenous people, and said that Columbus had had people hanged. Given these reports, the king and queen were concerned about the conditions in their New World colonies.

Still, the monarchs were not ready to abandon Columbus. They forced him to wait before he was granted an audience, but when they finally did see him, Isabella destroyed the papers filed in legal proceedings against him. He cried with relief at her loyalty.

The monarchs allowed Columbus, who was still convinced he had discovered the Indies, to return on a third voyage. By then, however, the king and queen had serious doubts about whether or not their new lands were actually near Asia at all.

Back to the New World

About this same time, Columbus met Amerigo Vespucci, a man from Florence, Italy, who worked in a company that supplied ships for extended voyages. Vespucci and Columbus had many conversations and quickly became friends.

When Columbus left Spain for his third voyage, he was more obsessed than ever with finding golden cities even though his health had deteriorated. He suffered from arthritis and gout, which is a very painful disease where crystals of uric acid form in the body's joints. Unknowingly, Columbus never avoided drinking alcohol or eating meat and seafood, all measures that would have helped prevent attacks of the disease. Even his eyesight was failing. Columbus had spent many days at sea staring at the horizon, close to the sun, for hours at a time. Now, his eyes were red and weepy, his vision blurry.

Yet he was not deterred. In fact, it was during this voyage that he made careful observations of nature. He, like others before him, realized the world was not a perfect sphere as the ancient

Greeks had claimed. He wrote, "I have seen so great an irregularity that, as a result, I have been led to hold this concerning the world, and I find that it is not round as they describe it, but that it is the shape of a pear."

Trouble in the Colonies

Chaos continued to dominate the settlement and the Spaniards that Columbus had left behind. Having abandoned La Isabela for a better site on the southern coast of Hispaniola, the colonists had a new settlement called Santo Domingo, named for Columbus's father. However, they were at war with each other as well as with the Native people. Columbus's brothers, Bartolomeo and Giacomo, had been unable to maintain order. Now that he had returned, neither could Columbus.

Because the colonists had lodged so many complaints against him, the monarchs sent men to collect Columbus and return him to Spain. Francisco de Bobadilla arrived on August 23, 1500, and seized control of the settlement and, in October, sent Columbus and his siblings home in chains.

He had fallen from grace. In October 1492, he had claimed his discovery for Spain, but within the span of eight years, Bobadilla returned the once-triumphant hero to the Spanish court as a shackled criminal. Columbus, now sick and nearly blind, was heartbroken. He returned to Spain blaming everyone else.

The king and queen were not gullible. They realized that, even if Columbus had enemies in their court, many of the reports about him had to be true. They knew that, no matter how much he blamed everyone around him, much of the responsibility for failure was his fault. When true leadership had been needed, Columbus had not been successful. The great sailor had been a terrible administrator.

Once again, the king and queen did not abandon Columbus. They gave him money and allowed him to keep most of his titles, but without the authority he was once allowed. He remained the Admiral of the Ocean Sea, but the power that went with it had vanished. The monarchs remained pleased that Columbus had made them king and queen of new lands, but they did not want to let him return there.

Instead, he worked feverishly to regain the royal trust he had once had. He knew that he could find Asia if he could only try once again. Yet the monarchs put him off. They appointed a new governor for the Indies, a nobleman named Don Nicolás de Ovando, and let him sail with additional colonists and provisions. He was ordered to retrieve Columbus's personal belongings and return them to Spain.

The Final Trip to the New World

After giving Ovando some time to establish his authority without Columbus's assistance, the monarchs finally allowed Columbus to travel across the sea for his fourth, and final, voyage. Columbus was forbidden by royal order to return to Santo Domingo, but he disobeyed. In part, he seems to have done so because he still felt he should have been in command there. He also wanted to warn Ovando about an approaching hurricane.

Ovando didn't believe Columbus and, as a result, twenty-five ships in his fleet were lost. Many people drowned. Afterward, Columbus left and explored the coastline of Panama. The ships he had with him, though, had been eaten by worms so badly that they were hardly seaworthy. They took on water even when the sailors manned the pumps. Finally, when Columbus's ships limped toward Jamaica's shore, Columbus had them run aground. They were lashed together and kept upright, but they could not be repaired. A chance rescue seemed impossible since there was so little regular ship traffic. It seemed the only course of action was to send Native people in canoes to Santo Domingo for help.

Nearly a year passed before rescue came. Finally, Columbus and his men were taken off the island of Jamaica. Most remained at Santo Domingo, but Columbus, his relatives, and his friends returned to Spain.

Bad news awaited him when he returned. Queen Isabella, who had supported him for many years, lay gravely ill. Within a few weeks, she died. Though she realized Columbus was not the man to govern the Indies, she remained faithful to him, assuring he received enough money to live richly. This alone was not enough to soften the blow of losing her presence at court, however. Columbus's final years were spent in Valladolid, a town in northern Spain, where he continued to petition the Spanish court for his original grants and titles. Although he was wealthy, he was unsatisfied because he had not achieved everything he had desired. His dreams of gold and glory had turned to dust.

Columbus's friends, including Vespucci, who had outfitted his third expedition, helped him as much as they could. Since Columbus's third voyage, Vespucci had made two of his own expeditions to South America—one for Spain and one for Portugal.

Some feel that Columbus and Vespucci must have been enemies. After all, people live in North and South America, not North and South Columbia. Vespucci was the first man to realize that what Columbus had discovered was not Asia, but North and South America. For this leap in the understanding of geography, mapmakers took to calling the new lands "America" in Vespucci's honor. Although some think Columbus was jealous because of this, it is doubtful that he was ever aware of it. The first known map that marks the New World as North and South America dates from 1507.

TRICKING THE NATIVE PEOPLE

While Columbus and his men were stranded on Jamaica, they found that the Native people there, once friendly, had become unwilling to deal with the Europeans. The skillful sailor, Columbus had one more trick up his sleeve: He told the Native people that God was angry with them. To prove it, he told them to watch the moon that night for a sign.

Columbus knew that there would be a lunar eclipse that night, a time when Earth's shadow covered the moon and made it fade from the night sky. Columbus anticipated this because he carried astronomical tables with him and was able to predict which night the eclipse would occur. The Native people did not know this, though, and were convinced that they had treated the Spaniards badly once they witnessed the eclipse. Columbus's son Ferdinand, who was along for the voyage, wrote in the biography *Life and Deeds*, "From that time forward they were diligent in providing us with all we needed."

Ultimately, Columbus's unhappiness kept him from realizing the true importance of what he had accomplished. He had opened up the New World for Spain, and the rest of Europe, to explore. He had brought back its riches, though they had been maize, tobacco, tomatoes, sweet potatoes, and tropical fruits, rather than mastic, gold, and cinnamon.

Columbus's discovery instigated others to travel the high seas, too. Within twenty years of Columbus's death, Ferdinand Magellan had **circumnavigated** Earth. New and better maps were being redrawn every year. Spanish colonies sprung up all over North America.

Amerigo Vespucci is credited with being the first European to realize that Columbus had not landed on Asia but instead discovered two entirely new continents. These two continents, North and South America, were named in his honor.

After centuries of assuming that the world was limited to Europe, Africa, and Asia, the people of Europe now knew that there were other lands and seas. Two additional continents had been added to their understanding, and they also now knew that there were multiple oceans as well. Thanks to the voyages of Christopher Columbus, Europeans had their eyes opened to a much larger world.

Columbus's Legacy

While Columbus had failed in his original quest to find an easterly route to Asia, what he did accomplish was far more significant. His opening up of the Americas to Europe would begin a significant number of changes to his world, as well as to the world he discovered.

A statue of Columbus in Barcelona, Spain. Although he spent the last years of his life in disgrace, Columbus is often memorialized for his achievement.

The Spanish exported many items and skills of their own to the Americas in what became known as the **Columbian Exchange**. The Spanish brought over horses, pigs, metalworking, sheep herding, coffee, and sugarcane. Both areas benefited from the exchange of food items, but not from the exchange of diseases from one continent to the other.

The Native people of the New World did not have any previous exposure to European diseases, including smallpox, influenza, measles, and the bubonic plague. Some people think that the common cold came from Europe, too, and was unknown in the Americas until after 1492. Millions of Native people died of these diseases and from poor treatment, even though the Spanish wanted to use them as slaves to work their gold mines. Slave labor became harder to find as many people died from European diseases. Several of Columbus's sailors returned from the Americas to Europe with a foreign malady as well, syphilis, a disease that would cause great misery for Europeans.

Widespread disease and Queen Isabella's disapproval of enslaving the Native people of the New World led to the import of Africans to Spain instead. Thus, slavery of Africans in the Americas began partly because the Spanish could not enslave the indigenous people who were sickly.

Spain felt the impact of Columbus's voyages. Taxes paid by Native people raised up to a fifth of the kingdom's annual income. King Ferdinand now had a place to send ambitious men who sought the sea. It was also safer for the Spanish monarch to allow Spain's criminals to sail to the New World. Thus, those who preferred to steal or kill for wealth were no longer a problem for Spanish authorities. The king could fearlessly ship criminals from Spain and never worry about them again.

Spain and Portugal, rivals when it came to exploiting the New World, agreed to divide it between them. The Treaty of Tordesillas (1494) gave the Spanish nearly exclusive rights to the New World, except for the eastward bulge of South America. Today, this is why people in Central and South America speak Spanish, except for those in Brazil, who speak Portuguese.

After Columbus's death, until the mid-twentieth century, he was hailed as a hero. Cities, rivers, and even a country were named for him. Just as people in the past didn't want to see

Protests against Christopher Columbus are common. Many view the Italian navigator as a criminal responsible for the destruction of Native American cultures.

anything bad he had done, some people today don't wish to recognize his achievements.

Columbus was a flawed man. Yet even in his obsession with the Indies and its wealth, and for all his inability to govern a colony, he had the heart of a devout man who wanted to convert indigenous people to Christianity. He made religious pilgrimages and often prayed. He maintained strong friendships with many people in Spain and some indigenous people, such as the Taíno chieftain. However, Columbus often failed to help the very people he wanted to befriend.

As we move into the twenty-first century, a complicated image of Columbus emerges. He was a courageous and talented sailor, but he was a terrible administrator who should have done more to maintain control over the Spanish colonists. He brought new, beneficial plants back to Europe and offered the Europeans the foods that have since shaped the culture of the Americas, but he carried just as many diseases to the New World from Europe.

Columbus died on May 20, 1506. Ferdinand, his son and biographer, wrote in *Life and Deeds* that he expired from "gout and other ills, and from grief at seeing himself so fallen from his high estate." Columbus achieved so much, yet his dreams of glory and limitless wealth were never fulfilled. Though rich in material things and money, he died unhappy, forgotten by his peers.

It is unlikely that the controversy surrounding Christopher Columbus is going to be settled any time soon. He is an endlessly complicated figure, responsible for one of the greatest events in the history of the world as well as some of its darkest moments. He was brave and boastful, ambitious and obsessive, adventurous and arrogant. In any event, the second Monday of October will continue to see a mix of celebration and protest of the legacy of Christopher Columbus.

Timeline

1451

Birth of Christopher Columbus in Genoa, Italy.

1476

Columbus is shipwrecked offshore of Lagos, Portugal.

1479

Columbus marries Felipa Perestrello Moniz.

1485

Columbus leaves Porto Santo, Portugal, for Palos, Spain.

1492

Columbus begins his first voyage and discovers the Bahamas, Cuba, and Hispaniola.

1493

Columbus returns to Palos, Spain.

1493–1496

Columbus leaves on second voyage and discovers Jamaica and Puerto Rico.

1494

Christopher Columbus founds La Isabela.

1496

Columbus reaches Portugal.

1498

Columbus leaves on third voyage.

1499–1500

Amerigo Vespucci's first voyage.

1500

Columbus is arrested and returned to Spain in chains. Vespucci is in the vicinity but will have nothing to do with the arrest.

1501–1502

Vespucci's second voyage.

1502

Columbus leaves on his fourth voyage.

1503

Columbus beaches ships on Jamaica.

1504

Columbus returns to Spain.

1506

Christopher Columbus dies in Valladolid, Spain.

Glossary

caravel A small, sturdy ship used by the Spanish to explore the New World, popularized by Prince Henry the Navigator.

Catholicism Also called Roman Catholicism, a Christian religious sect that derives its organization and authority from the Pope in Rome.

Columbian Exchange The term for the exchange of food, animals, cultures, technologies, diseases, and people between Europe and the Americas as a result of European exploration.

circumnavigate To travel all the way around something, especially by water.

colonize To send a group of settlers to a place to establish political control over it.

dead reckoning A system of figuring out a ship's location by noting time and distance from port.

genocide The deliberate elimination of mass groups of people by killing them.

Indies A term that in Columbus's day referred to an area that included India and all of eastern Asia, including Cipango and Cathay. Today, the "West Indies" refers to the group of islands between the southeastern shores of the United States and the northern shores of South America.

latitude The distance north or south of the equator.

longitude The distance east or west of a given point. In Columbus's time, it was not possible to determine longitude.

mastic An aromatic and expensive resin from a tree on the island of Chios that is used for perfume and medicine.

Moors The term for Muslims originating from northwestern Africa who conquered Spain in the eighth century and who were driven out in the fifteenth century.

Muslim A member of the religious faith of Islam, which was founded in the seventh century by the Prophet Muhammad, who is believed to have had a moral code revealed to him by the god Allah.

nao A merchant ship, larger than a caravel but not nearly as sturdy or fast.

Ocean Sea The term for the Atlantic Ocean prior to the discovery of other oceans; prior to Columbus's voyage, the known world (including Europe, Asia, and Africa) were thought to be surrounded by one large ocean.

pagan A general term for non-Christians.

Renaissance A intense period of artistic, literary, and scientific curiosity beginning in Italy and lasting roughly from the fourteenth to the sixteenth century.

trade winds Constant winds useful for sailors. The northeast trade winds, which Columbus used, flow from the Canary Islands to the Caribbean.

tribute A payment made from one group of people subject to the power of another group of people.

For More Information

Books

Bartosik-Velez, Elise. *The Legacy of Christopher Columbus in the Americas: New Nations and a Transatlantic Discourse of Empire.* Nashville, TN: Vanderbilt University Press, 2014.

Irving, Washington. *The Life and Voyages of Christopher Columbus.* Charleston, SC: Bibliolife, 2009.

Loewen, James W. *Lies My Teacher Told Me About Christopher Columbus: What Your History Books Got Wrong.* New York, NY: The New Press, 2014.

McKay, Rodney. *Christopher Columbus 61 Success Facts— Everything You Need to Know about Christopher Columbus.* Queensland, Australia: Emereo Publishing, 2014.

Websites

Discover Columbus's Ships
www.thenina.com/index.html
The Columbus Foundation maintains two replica ships of the *Niña* and the *Pinta* that serve as a sailing museum.

The History Channel: Christopher Columbus
www.history.com/topics/exploration/christopher-columbus
The History Channel's page on Christopher Columbus contains a thorough biography of his life as well as videos related to his voyages.

The Mariner's Museum: Christopher Columbus
ageofex.marinersmuseum.org/index.php?type=explorer&id=12
Explore the routes Columbus traveled during his voyages; take a closer look at his ships and their tools of navigation.

Index